"EVERETT HOAGLAND'S IS THE POETRY OF REGISTERED EXPERIENCE,

of sharpened perception rationalized into poetic "use" of great effectiveness. What he speaks of through ironies, delineates, derogates, praises. These are crystallized self-revelations, emotionally powered, intellectually burnished, self-possessions of a sensibility still searching for the fullest clarity of Who, What, Where, Why?

A clarity in and of the world, which, as it effloresces with each new work, beats sound-word-image like the log of a very old say-lore (griot-french) Djali, like the most ancient poets' 'Glee Club.' It's how we have raised the sun, each AM, from Osiris, through Orpheus: Douglass and DuBois and Langston and Zora and Sterling and Margaret and Jimmy and Lorraine and Henry Dumas and Them.

Or Roumain, Mikey Smith, Guillen, Neruda and Them. All Them Thems is We. One of Them Thems is Hoagland. Hoagland makes us remember to Shine. Which is our write-ful name!"
—Amiri Baraka

"Every person in the world stands in need of a poet/friend, someone who cares and someone who comprehends. Everett Hoagland is just such a poet/friend. I sure am glad he's mine."
—Maya Angelou

...Here...

...Here...

New and Selected Poems

by

Everett Hoagland

With a Foreword by
Martín Espada

Leapfrog Press
Wellfleet, Massachusetts

Published in 2002 in the United States by
The Leapfrog Press
P.O. Box 1495 95 Commercial Street
Wellfleet, MA 02667-1495, USA
www.leapfrogpress.com
info@leapfrogpress.com

Distributed in the United States by
Consortium Book Sales and Distribution
St. Paul, Minnesota 55114
www.cbsd.com

First Edition

Library of Congress Cataloging-in-Publication Data

Hoagland, Everett.
    Here : new and selected poems / by Everett Hoagland ; with an introduc-
tion by Martin Espada.— 1st ed.
        p. cm.
    ISBN 0-9679520-5-0 (alk. paper)
    1. African Americans—Poetry. I. Title.
    PS3558.O335 H47 2002
    811'.54—dc21

2002000612

I am grateful for the assistance of Denise G. Rebeiro who typed and retyped and
retyped the manuscript for this book. The skills, time, and patience she gave to
the project were extraordinary and are very much appreciated.

With eternal love for my mother,
Estelle Johnson Hoagland, 1918 – 195 ,

who introduced me to the spirituals,
Paul Robeson's singing,
Duke Ellington's music,
and the Philadelphia Orchestra,

who read to me from Aesop's Fables,
the fables of Uncle Remus, The Bible,
and from a world of poetry, and
who equipped me with pre-kindergarten
literacy.

Here, dear heart, are more "flowers."

Acknowledgments

Some of the poems in this collection first appeared in and are selected from the following publications. Grateful acknowledgment is hereby made to the editors/publishers of the publications.

Periodicals

The American Poetry Review
The Beloit Poetry Review
Black World
Caliban
Communications Education
Compass
Discover America: San Jose Studies
Essence
First World
The Iowa Review
Longshot
The Massachusetts Review
The Progressive
The Southcoast Insider
The New Bedford Standard Times
Temper: The UMass Dartmouth Review
World: The Journal of The Unitarian Universalist Association
XCP: Cross Cultural Poetics

Chapbooks

Ten Poems
Black Velvet
Suite: Sister
Scrimshaw

Anthologies

The Black Poets
Patterns
The New Black Poetry
New Black Voices
Significance: The Struggle We Share
Giant Talk

The Jazz Poetry Anthology
The Garden Thrives: Twentieth Century African American Poetry
The Body Electric: The Best Poetry from the American Poetry
   Review, 1972-1999
Drumvoices Revue: Summer/Fall 2000

Book

   This City and Other Poems

Contents

Foreword   13
Preface / Poem   17

CELEBRATION

At East/West Beaches   23
Celebration   24
Umoja   29
Homecoming   30
Of the African Eve   33
Rosebud   36
Good Bloods and Bad Water   39
Talking Shit: King Leopold's Voice Box   40
Gorée   42
Dust   46
The Seven Days   47
In the Boston MFA   48

THE MUSIC

Legacies   53
On Free Will and The Rights Of Man   57
Keeping The Faith   60
The Music   62
The Last Scottsboro "Boy"   64
Big Zeb Johnson   66
For Joanne Little   68
Fired Up!!   72
Impromptu: After The Call   74
Georgia On His Mind   76
Red, White And Blues Country   77
J + 12   79
Kinda Blue: Miles Davis Died Today   80
The Bones And Dust Of The Poet   82
Bob Kaufman?   84
you should be shoo be   87
Puttin' On The Dog   93
Attitude Adjustment   95
The In-Dex   96

To Be Or Not To Be   98
Dominion   101
Undoing The Do   102
Pop Pop   104
. . . Here . . .   105

AT THE ACCESS

Occasionally   109
The Moose: First Sighting   112
At The Access   114
The Pilgrim   116
. . . Unfinished . . .   118

The Author   121

Foreword

Reading the poems of Everett Hoagland is akin to being in the presence of a great teacher. This is the teacher who, it seems, has read everything, has seen and heard everything, and who shares everything in such a way that the student never forgets. Indeed, there is a generosity and an integrity in these poems, a commitment to word and principle, characteristic of the best teachers. From them we learn history or politics, to be sure, but also how to think and feel and live in the world. This thirty-year compendium of poems from Everett Hoagland teaches and teaches.

The people crowding these poems might spring from a vast mural of African and African-American history. We see Sally Hemings, the slave mistress of Thomas Jefferson; the last of the Scottsboro "Boys," falsely accused and imprisoned for rape, but still free of hate; Joann Little, a prison inmate who killed the white guard attempting to rape her; the Beat poet Bob Kaufman; jazz trumpeter Miles Davis, on the occasion of his death; Winnie Mandela, the wife of Nelson Mandela, who fell from grace in South Africa. Aside from the famous and the infamous, we also meet Nate Shaw, an unknown sharecropper who told his extraordinary life story in the book *All God's Dangers;* anonymous slaves and their descendants on Gorée Island; and the nameless victims of "King Leopold's Voice Box," a diabolical instrument used in the Belgian Congo to coerce Africans into speaking French.

The poet's own family ghosts stare at us from the vast mural too, like his great-grandfather, William David Holmes, a soldier in the Union Army, and extended family like his maternal grandmother's ancient, ex-slave friend, miz green—who knitted Hoagland's baby bonnet as a gift to his grandmother, and to his mother when she was pregnant with him during America's first year in World War Two—with her "shiny crinkled / black ribbon keloid scars right / up there to the neck where / master had whipped her sunday morning / on the way to church for burning / breakfast biscuits." The image, like the scars, is indelible.

Everett Hoagland speaks and sings for them all. He speaks and sings for the black man in the poem "Georgia on His Mind:"

> His tongue is cotton;
> his mind a cotton gin;
> his life a mill wheel on

13

the river, oils the machine.

His soul is a boll weevil.

He is a poet of the defiant. But he is also a poet of the dejected, the despairing, the ones with boll weevil souls. Damaged people are always with us, and almost always invisible, but when the poet tells us that their souls are boll weevils, we suddenly see them, and cannot forget them. They have human faces though they may have larva-stage souls. Yet history affirms that those larvae-souls could escape the cropped bolls of slavery, sharecropping, jim crow, unemployment, or criminal injustice, to rise and fly through blues, like Ray Charles' "Georgia," to self-acceptance, to some kind of gritty, self-mocking reconciliation with black life's all too frequent unfair and oppressive circumstances.

Everett Hoagland is a poet who speaks and sings of the dust. He understands that, "We are dust. . . . Its stuff will not / make good statues of your heroes. / Heroes are made of it. . . . Explosives never destroy it. / It cannot be slung or thrown. / Primitive / but it can kill you." He searches for signs of humanity in the dust, driven by an acute sensitivity to human suffering and the struggle against it. He cannot stand at the edge of a lake without wondering "who walked in, fell in, jumped in, went / under to lake bed long ago."

The title of the collection, *Here*, is revealing. Everyone in these poems is here, with us, now. History is here; the ancestors are here, not in some vague abstract sense, but with immediate clarity, summoned by the poet. Their labors, their sacrifices, their languages and music, their legacy, still have real daily consequences for all of us.

When the poet Pablo Neruda died in September 1973, his funeral became the first demonstration against Chile's murderous military junta. Some mourners in the march cried out: "¡Compañero Pablo Neruda!" Others answered: "¡Presente!" *Here.* Those who cried out, and those who answered them, risked their lives to tell the world that a dead man was still alive. Neruda was and is here.

That is the same *here* of Everett Hoagland's poems. Angry, celebratory, incantatory, there is a presence in these poems that will not be denied. The poet is here, and he is a teacher. Learn from him.

Martín Espada
Amherst, Massachusetts
December 2001

. . .Here. . .

Preface / Poem

". . . of . . . historical hangovers
. . . literary cornflakes . . . university
corners of tailored intellect
& universal anesthesia. . . ."
—from "ON" by Bob Kaufman

here's to you too
who have had the power
and the glory authority
will for:

rugazi
vieques
chiapas
foco
sarajevo
east timor
kosovo
tiananmen square
hebron
burundi
phnom penh
my lai
soweto
no gun ri
hiroshima
unit 731
camp van dorn
auschwitz
krystalnacht
tulsa
rosewood
reservations
wounded knee
middle

passage

tenochtitlan you
who among columbus' crew hacked
off arms of unarmed
arawak diseased the carib

you who inquisited crusaded
who colored history
with sex race blood
encoded things
whites called other
people — black red yellow mulat-
toes negroes mestizos — you name it

you who rent spent minds
by paying muddled middle
men and women to buy into
today's all
right with the right
wing diversion of consciousness
"movement" called multiculturalism

this all fluff and no stuff
in
insubstantial apolitical
subversion of
substitute for

real change for chump change
given to neatly tied and bowed
new hanker-
chief head-n.i.c. bosses

who in turn push it
on us covered with
the mass printed
multicolored dots
on an airtight wonder

bread wrapper
for some cotton
candy semblance

of the staff of life mass
starved folk fight

and for what
should a poet write about all
the bread cooled out sopped up
bloods and other

"minorities"

are making off with getting off on this new off-
setting of our ongoing
right on
collective human rights

struggles' multicultural
bag that is about as universal
as a eurocentric university
lit. crit. scene

nixed "mixed" blood
cop baton beaten
bop beat
poet
bob

kaufman might say
read "ON"

CELEBRATION

At East/West Beaches

The day night was born
we searched for time
and sea-smoothed fragments of blue, green,

brown bottles. Glass
cleared of gloss
made of man-and-woman-made
fire and sand made from stone
made from rock made
from cosmic dust. We

fringed the lips of under-
tow with footprints the waves
redeemed from the firm, wet
shore. We gathered and gave each other
milk white moonstones, aeons
old obsidian, pebbles
translucent as sucked rock
candy and rolled up our jeans in the raw

salty mist. The sun sank into
a violet-lipped quahog, and grit-edged night
opened like a mussel. Under
lacquered, pearly black
light of moonrise we crossed
over a sandbar
into camp ground by
duned, scrub
beach rose.

The night day was born
we turned around and found
no footprints.

Celebration

1.

Lest we forget

every Fourth of July
I want some country, some-
one to send a replica of one of all
those slave ships over the Middle
Passage to the tall ship parade—
to keep it honest, to make it real, to see. . . .

Remember them
moored in mind at the waterfront steps
of Newport's storied mansions?

. . . From under the Mt. Hope Bridge
with haunting hurricanes in their wakes,
came the Portuguese *Sangue*, the Spanish, French, Dutch, Danish,
English and Yankee entries,
Then slowly, slowly, slowly as as-
similation, civil rights
came the *Lord Ligonier*, with a hold full
of *Roots*, after the *Esperanza* and *Jesus*
and with a cargo of allusive scrimshaw

on human bones. . . .

A tide of blood recedes
exposing skeletons
and hand-carved bone crosses
pressed in the middle of Bibles
and history books.

2.

Sister Love bops beside me.

We embrace as history and future. We

walk along and down
but not away from the "Deep River"
we sing of, ". . . *loud as the rolling sea. . . .*"

She smiles all over
home where the blues are
somewhere between the greens
and the cornbread. Love

as bread
cast upon the waters. . . .

Let us break bread together
on our knees, on our knees
Let us break bread together
on our knees.

3.

Cook! Sing the song Sister!!

Blood's in this cornbread
corn in the bread Baby
sun in the corn a son of
Africa in the cornucopia eyes
looking this way you
rite a bread
with dough so blushed with song
baked hot with mandated melanin
requisite to taste
this place's air

There is a pestle and gourd about
the act of kneading the tacky ova
of grain stained with sun

Your cornbread gets down
in the shiny baking pan
is a tambourine to glory
up into the oven as germ to womb . . .

black eyed peas
swell as syphons of the sauce
distilled from a swine whose funky soul
sacramentally
dances in the potted primal ooze and
around in his own severed feet and side-
steps as bacon drippins in the chorus of collards
on the amen corner of the stove
holy rollin'
'cause cookin' is a kind of dance done
with the hands and heart
your stone-ground stirrin' counter-shakes
it makes it fecund and arousin'
it is hotly kissed by fire bakes
it and we takes it. . . .

4.

. . . sweet baked apple dappled
cinnamon speckled
nutmeg freckled
peach brandy and amber wine
woman
WOW
with your pipin' hot
finger poppin' black
african pepper pot
not stoppin' steamin'
coffee flowin' creamin' brown
sugar growin' cane candy
comin' cocoa
goin' crazy
'bout brown sugar teases
GOOD GOD
and pleases
SWEET JESUS
that honey stained soul trained
slow molasses ass
HOTDAMN
candied yam and sweet potato pie

thighs
sweet raisin tipped coconuts
raisin' cane
sugar
stone brown sugar bowl belly
TO THE BONE
TO THE BONE. . . .

5.

. . . At the beach
by the seeded ring cove
she lay back, unbuttoned her
maternity blouse, knees funneled
moonsky and sea. Above
the sandbar there was a gold
ring around the moon. Stretch marks
rippled from her navel
cameo of time; tributaries flowed down around
her full-womb-stretched skin.

Moonlight unrolled
ancient scrolls of water
containing Middle
Passage names
and her water broke
with Nia.

Nia, when they put you
bloody and immaculate
on your mother's diaphanous
abdomen,
you kneaded your shadow;
love stared milk and your mother cooed

awe, Now

you cry for beamed moon juice
in this dark room.

Nia, Nia, Nia, Nia.
Herispapa' spoopoo;
herishimfudgepudge: Nia,
plump and healthy on your Mama's mana
smile, I pronounce your name.

Purpose I pronounce your blood-red name
as your mother suckles you,
rocking in a bentwood chair built like
bop, smiling crescent moons.

Umoja

We put our infant daughter Nia
to sleep nestled, suckled, sated
three seats inside the hollow aisle
of the jumbo jet.

High over the Atlantic Ocean, flying through
the night to Dakar, "The Paris of Africa,"
the capital of Negritude, flying back
with implicit faith in what is
flying us home through time zones over
human bones under the Middle Passage,
the deep dark outside the plane's star-scratched
windowpanes, holding hands all night to land,
at breaklight, at the place from where
all our dawns have come.

The jet's shadow comes at a coastal fishing
village like a shark. We step off the
angled plane onto ancestral soil to see
our footprints in the same deep red dust
our people have worked in Jersey, Georgia
and Jamaica. The dust of drought surrounds
Dakar like a goopher or vévé.

At N'Gor, the sea-side resort,
we are served kola nuts and palm wine
in calabashes while hired hands play
kora and khalam and room keys exchange
hands and hands exchange soul shakes.

*The Pan African Writers' Association
World Poetry Festival,
University of Ghana, Legon
November, 1999*

Homecoming

*"Do ba-na co-ba, gene me, ge-ne me!
Do ba-na co-ba, gene me, ge-ne me!"*

*"Do ba-na co-ba, gene me, ge-ne me!
Do ba-na co-ba, gene me, ge-ne me!"* *

we who are
american made who
feel and act like we are
making it in america

ensconced in mansions
with yachts
and other leisure craft
sometimes forget last

time we crossed

over the atlantic we
had to
we had

. . . we . . .

were so many too
few to . . . by twos
by the score in lots sold
singly or by the dirty dozens

baptized by inhumanity
in the name of the slaveship
in the name of our "owners"
and the power and the glory
of their successive sons many thousand-
thousands did not make it

. . . gone . . .

we who are american made
who act and feel like we
have it made in america some-

times forget

his craft and power are great
and still armed with steel gray greed
and hate that enforce foreign policy
begun with middle

passage forgive

the heavy air this plaint
brings to our affair
here you see
my great-grandparents' grandparents
came from somewhere in the old gold coast

indulge me you see the last time
the we in me crossed the sea
sickened naked branded we barely
made it we

traveled so lightly forgive
this funk those of us who
were not sick and jettisoned
like junk survived to make

possible succeeding amber waves of we
who currently seem to have it made
in america had seaborne ancestors
who in me are just recently airborne

here who

endured floggings and rapes in the name
of moral and cultural superiority who
bore up under ten stone bales of cotton
who rose in negro spirituals from christenings

in their own blood from baptismals awash
with their urine vomit liquid feces and pus
and walked free of the heavy air of the hold
into the sea-deep blues of american slavery

and its legacies pardon them
for returning in mixed company in me
for returning so ponderously my air
is heavy because I am here for them

fresh out of the funky hold of america
in the name of their lost forgotten family
chained names thrown overboard or other-
wise drowned in troubled water named nameless
middle passage cape fear river "negroes"
gone
down in holy water drowned to be reborn
from kofi to cuffee to cousins
flourishing somewhere among the humanity

here i am

distant family extended nearly to the point
of no return but not as had been hoped for
by the slave breakers not beyond endurance
beyond belief for by-and-by by real miracles

of rebellion escape cross-
overcoming by bullets ballots births
beliefs blessings
they are here in me
by invitation
by way of high john
hambone ring shouts jazz and pan
african airways

"Do ba-na co-ba, gene me, ge-ne me!
Ben-de nu-li, nuli, nuli, ben-de le" *

* *from chapter 14, "The Souls of Black Folk" by W. E. B. DuBois.*

Of the African Eve

so now *they* see it
as clearly as we
saw the dogon binary star
they at first could not see

but which we knew
was there though they
said it could not be be-
cause they had not seen it

just as the great african water-
fall was unnamed nonexistent
until livingston
saw it named it after
victoria to keep it
from going native and indians

already there did not discover
the americas christ-
opher columbus did
in the name of spain
and the power and the glory
forever

now they say african woman was
is more than mammae
fire maker wood and water bearer
they acknowledge eden was
and mother africa is

more than myth or metaphor
for what we had already read
in the rock and drum roll record
of her hip music in the rosetta

stone hard fact of her eons
old footprint and kente cloth
weave of her in all our dna
they say she was and is

much more than victim more
than earth
mother she is more
than isis aphrodite madonna
even more than eve
more than the side-show hottentot
venus of their bustle-shaped envy's
scorn
more than the butt of history
more than plied middle

passage of taken pleasure but
they still don't see
their telling redundancy:
their "eve" was african

she is who
now declares her-
self owns shares her history
she who has carried

a continent on her head
the whole human race swaddled
on her back "the slave's slave"
laborer's laborer bearer's bearer

once caged by adam's ribs
indeed today she is she
who now writes wrongs
unites human rights

with softback novels'
bone hard ribbing
she who everyone came out of
through concentric cervixes

we are she
is us
we are
because she was
they say everything is

relative so now it seems
is everyone some by blood
just thinly kin many thousand
thousands times removed others

more immediately sisters
brothers we must apple-
ogize for our oppressive
myths for our hard ribbing

about adam let us celebrate
her in the afterlife of liberating
words in deeds mindful of the milky way
of her millions years upright heartdrum

dance around the world
today with a myth called science
they say that all our ancestors came
out of her and walked around

an edenic africa and
throughout the world
on ice
in rain forest
among mountains
across wide windy plains
all children

of an african "eve"
we said it long ago *but*
now *they* say it so
it must be
so

Rosebud

brothers fathers
orson wells raised kane
we too can
end the inhumane pain
that reigns in the name
of culture

show with poems music
films paintings
dances sculpture
there must be

NO

more nip-
ping cut
-ting off under-
developed woman-
hood the pink
pearls enveloped in petals
of terminal budded girls

the ages of all those
stone altered virgins gone
to dust sacrificed for sun
colored mahiz by aztec
priests please

STOP

cropping their sex their
capacity for full-bloomed
pleasure with preused rusty
indifference jagged edged
razor silence there
must be

NO

clit-
oridectomies:
the ultimate act of misogyny

—except for bride burnings
  in parts of love
  templed india where
  to some hymens sums seem
  more important than humans
  like all those newborn
  girls in china lake
  drowned for sons—

bouquets of cut roseflesh
long-stemmed black buds
in bloodfilled vases
by virtue
of "tradition"

with the prying
fingers pruning
hands of equally
complicit males
and traditional fe-
males in a self-righteous
rite of man-made mind
maiming pain beyond belief
in in-
fectious deaths

(*in the family name of chastity?*)

let her be
all of herself

DON'T

violate her on the altar
of power and glory
forever in the name
of a godhood erected
in the image of malekind

nor alter nor lessen
the sanctity of her
body she needs to be
completely self-

determined to keep or share
all or any parts of her
freely by human rights
her life's work is more than being
merely bearer of wood water pain

children and imposition more than
just being dutiful daughter sister mother wife
freedom fighter poets writers artists fight
for her right to be as much of all

of herself as she was born with
and can be
-come

Good Bloods and Bad Water

One must scorn the air-conditioned hotel
for the local Wolof musicians to take you out
to a ghetto of Dakar, French style,
worse than home. You relearn
how to eat sun-dried fish, rice,
couscous, cassava by hand

from friendly, giving folk who rename you,
when you squat with them around
a circular communal dinner pot
in a square room of the horizontal
tenement, where the water is polluted
by the drainage from tourist hotel sewage pipes

you smell the fruit of negritude. In the Palace
of Politics the smiling ebony persona of France pours rosé
on the scarlet royal carpet, "For our
ancestors." On the other side
of the guarded wrought iron fence bars
of those elegantly caged in the villanelle,
in the three unities, the barely living
poor, our true hosts, drink foul water—

to kora, khalam and balafon.

Talking Shit: King Leopold's Voice Box*

Vous parlez Français très bien!
Vous parlez très bien!

Well, when I was young
they would lynch your language,
hang your mother tongue.

En Français! En Français! They say.

When you speak your words,

Mistake! They say.
They bring out a box,
big enough to hold
your head,
have it filled with human feces,
called it The Black Voice Box.*

Hang it from your neck, just

beneath your chin.
Watch your tears fall in it
with a righteous grin.
When you get the speech *'right'*
They have it taken

away.

To fill it up fresh for mistakes

the next day. They tried
to turn our talking into
a canal
of flowing French.

Yes, 'the tongue is the customer of the ear,' **

but here, it was also
the slave of the nose, forced
laborer, the bearer
of dripping, paisley
tears.

A "learning" device, used by teaching priests and nuns, in what were the French and Belgian Congos. This is from testimony by a Franco-phone African survivor at the "Beyond Negritude: Contemporary Thought in the Franco-phone World" Conference, Brown University, November, 1988.

** *An African proverb.*

Gorée

". . . necessary and inevitable
like the 'inevitable' slave past
through consciousness like the present. . . ."
from "The Path of the Stars" by Augustino Neto

Gorée ten miles off shore beckons
from the western horizon like the landscape
of the troubled dream and we sleepwalk to the ferry.

Twenty thousand-thousand gone through the Gorée trade alone
we are told.

This is a Catholic isle off a Moslem land.
This the church where truth was chained.
Here Jesus died and rose again.
The beads we say are knots of blood.
Here they force-fed us after the trek in chains.
Here men were sold by size, nubile women penned
and prized for comeliness. Mulattoes conceived here,
and their mothers, were boated back to the main-
land to buffer tides of rage. Here children's
chains are sold as souvenirs; they anchor history
and the mind. Here they took, selected the best;
the rest: lame, old, small and sick were helped
to die.

The writing is on the stockade walls: poster sized
revolutionary rhetoric, Pan-African credos, race
pride logos, reminders, challenges and warnings
written in black by the descendants
of the survivors of the dried blood red walls
of the pastel colonial buildings'
shuttered silence.

We've had to come all the way
back to see, clearly poetry kill people, blind them,
cause them to cough blood and be crippled
in a French provincial palace of mind,

with a court, an overmonied ten percent
of the population, prospering lords and ladies,
fronting masks. Eighty percent of each dollar spent
on the slave factory island, on a ROOTS tee shirt
goes to France. *"See Your Roots"* cotton
shirts off bony backs are hawked by hungry hustlers
inside the barracoon's walls. Bloods at its
doors trade cowry shells for your money or
urge on you a brand new djuju bag –

for fifty Central African francs.

At sunset on Gorée Island, where scavenging
brown hawks wheel above the huge metal cross
atop the island's highest point, the volcano
sleeps silent as the broken cannon pointed there
over the Middle Passage. . . .
down a long dark corridor a doorless doorway
to the past and future opens
to the surf's wash and soft thud on the black
boulders. The blue-eyed horizon of this eastern shore . . . gone.
You are your shadow silhouetted in the rectangular
frame that is the grave of time, where so much went
underground. You had to, had to, you
had to come all the way back
to the rock fortress, to the slave pens,
get down
on your hands and knees and crawl into
the stone oven of a cell
where the African rebels' yell and defiance were kept
in solitary. Compressed by silence and circumstance
to diamond-hard blues. Completely black
inside the cell alone, one sees and hears things
clearly in the deep darkness. Overhead are heard
the voices of African-American tourists
calling their mates to, "Come look at this
Tyree. Come see this Dee. . . ." One hears a sea
of twenty thousand thousand voices at once

but also this from the shadows that always crowd
your view-finder, even in the dark:

"Do you tan? The native women are
charming. Does he take Master Charge? How
can they be so resigned? Gee, Gorée is neat fun!"
inside the cowry shell you hold to your ear
you hear your name and heartbeat;
you finger the humming walls of the
cubicle and chip the tactile darkness
for a keepsake to put in your
djuju bag: ancient black lava rock.

You crawl out into the light
of the setting sun, face the western horizon
and, stripping as you go, hanging your watch
and jeans, western shirt and shoes on your white
shadow, you wade into
the east shore of the Middle Passage—
the hyphen between African
and American—
the surf hisses and steams off you
like water around white hot iron.
You walk out farther, level with your
heart. Farther, until the edge of life
is just over your head. You hold your
breath under water, open your eyes, clench
your fists and let the bellow bubble out
of you.
But you bound off the sand and obsidian
bottom and beat your breath back to the surface. . . .

As we board the ferry back to Dakar
the ghosts of twenty million swarm the wharf;
waifs with open palms and eyes closed by
disease and blindness, with ringworm in their
rusty dreadlocks, beg
for fifty Central African francs.

The Paris of Africa.

At sunset, the sea around Gorée is red;
it recedes revealing twenty thousand-
thousand gone and western rigs drilling

offshore for new black gold.

Later, alone in the bush, squatting
at the base of an ashy baobab, you contemplate
it all: your blue jeans,
the same old cotton, under
the same old sun,
the same old so-called "communes,"
the same old mules,
the same gaunt shadows lengthening
in the light. And how
oppression always
smells the same, looks the same, how
poverty personified is always full
of the same self
hate and hospitality.

You look at, listen to
the little whirlwinds, dust devils
swirling on the dry red road
and think of goopher,
think of vévé.
You take a twig and score
your name under a poem
you are able to read in the deep
red dust:

Dust

We are dust.

Rock is the placenta of time.
But rock can be shattered.

You cannot break dust;
it defies the hammer.
Chisels cannot carve up-

on it. Its stuff will not
make good statues of your heroes.
Heroes are made of it. Blown up?
Explosives never destroy it.
It cannot be slung or thrown.
Primitive

but it can kill you.

The Seven Days

We return through customs wearing the ebony
Seven Days' masks haggled for at the barracoon
beach boutique. Seven days carved as
masks we carry through time and customs.
Beneath the ebony stain, they are grained
like all the lifelines of a family's
hands. A blue-eyed redhead at the customs gate
says,

Welcome home!

He checks all but the seven days
and the djuju bag I wear around my neck.
It holds: seed, black stone, red dust, root slice
of the baobab, a seashell from the east
shore of the deep hyphen between African
and American. We are returned to this
departure point, without our shadows,
with that which is discovered with loss,
with that which is lost with discovery.

In the Boston MFA

There is an exhibit in Paris to spotlight the fact
that much art stolen by Nazi officers still has not
been returned to surviving owners and rightful heirs.
—CBS News

There is no "African Art
In Motion Contexts".* What is a mask
without the masque? Dogon, Akan, Wolof
Bapende, Senufo, Maconde, Baga, Bambara:

What is a mask without drum
music, without the moving man or woman
within,
without the dance
without the prayer
or song???? Raised silence.

A still and quiet *bas relief*, a genteel museum
peace, hung just so, like "Strange Fruit."
Does dance hang on a wall?
Can prayer and song be shelved?

(But song needs silences to be musical.
Prayer needs silence to be heard.
The word needs silhouetting silence.)

Even so, artful Grande Acquisitors, brahmin
grave robbers, shrine desecrators, by degrees,
these are death
masks of copped cultures:

Inca copper, turquoise, jewelry,
Aztec gold and emerald jaguars
(they could not mine the sunshine, the light
or shadow of the undulating stone Mayan pyramidal
snake.) Stone-tongues
alabaster Babylonian tombstones, semi-
abstract African masks, attesting

to the manifests
of Manifest Destiny's slave-
ships, galleons and Conestoga wagons:
the fine art of holocaust, after holocaust, after. . . .

What is a mask?

The ghost masks of genocide are sleep
walking, homeless, addled, idle, turned
around, street talking to themselves in Roxbury,
Dorchester, their
lives somnambulant undeferred nightmares
up and down Blues Hill Ave.

What is a mask?

They are other-
wise god-images still.

Listen

across the deep
spiritual river renamed,
The Charles. After
spirited entreaties, recently returned English
ivy-covered Lakota
skulls warehoused at Harvard
returned to their context

in earth and prayer
in dance and dust
in smoke and sky
in the way the dead are meant
to come alive: masked
in motion and in memory.

A lecture/presentation by Robert Farris Thompson.

THE MUSIC

Legacies

"The day of 'aunties,' 'uncles,'
and 'mammies' is equally gone. . . ."
— *Alain Locke*

in sleep some long dead come to me
and crown my head with fine hand-knit
blues that were the overpaid dues back
then of those who hoped and willed me
heirloomed free by any black and bloody
green liberation dreams necessary:

in the kitchen of a family
house no longer there
in the friends' city of brotherly love that never was
gathered around my long dead
maternal grandma mama
wawa's coal stove where her
deeply silent antebellum-born old
folk neighbors helped themselves to her
strong warming everpresent
coffee sweetened lightened like
our 'tis of thee history
with sugar and cream she asked
ancient café solo miz green to unfasten
the back of her long high mary lincoln-like
dress so my late mother late
aunts back
in their late nineteen-teens early
twenties girlhoods could stare as shiny crinkled
black ribbon keloid scars right
there up to her neck where
master had whipped her sunday morning
on the way to church for burning
breakfast biscuits making them
unbearable insufferable overbrowned
unfit for sopping up the once over easy

egg yolks he liked with linked blood
sausage fritters and fries under
the understanding eyes of his good
first family females fair
ladies who graced the waiting carriage
until his rightful husbanding hand had
ended the exercise of the power
and glory of their chivalrous kind and
returned the whip to their relatively well
groomed groom "uncle" ned whose

eyes bled staring
at his lacerated mutilated
barely conscious naked
little daughter being
attended to by his black coffee-brown
broom-jump wife "aunt" dammy
the carriage lurched as they started for church
when the lead horse
(with anxious knowing blindered eyes)
was first stung by the bloody tip of the whip
the chastened girl survived to become
another auntie to similarly genteel
old dominion gentry whose hand-me-down
consciences calloused from such
commonplace displays of superiority

a slave ship manifest
destiny of those who survived being bought sold out-
right raped who
lived to be
aunts themselves to non-kin
as such called out of forgotten
african family names drowned in holy water
by labels designed to make them
nurses nurturers of their privileged oppressors
but armed like sojourner with wit
will with the moral authority of a madonna
and by-and-by by brains
by bullets ballots

counterreigns of belief
many an awesome auntie outgrew the brand
name and namer and becomingly became
herself
many thousand wiled and smiled them-
selves off the jemima pancake mix box many
thousand gone from nameless graves
stare and smile
down from over
the battlements of God's glory
down on dearly crowned descendents
who name their progeny accordingly
in the green suburbs of their promised land
whose blessings stream from dreams
steeped in black mammae milk

nearly one hundred antebellum child cook
miz green's big knuckled man-sized hands
made my superb little light
weight blue baby bonnet
back in nineteen forty-two when dark blue
green night shades on our living
room windows were drawn to keep the war far and
away the finest tight knit of personal worth
by extended family i
have seen just last year my late mother
said . . . here . . . and handed it
over and over again i am
reminded of the demeaning
mean-nothing-by-it legacy
out of long memory deep
as those who sleep late
in middle passage seabed
those who were
lashed with a tongue forked
like the liberty bell's
knells steepled recall
steeped in blood and dream
anti-auntie-bellum legacies heard
in chronic words that call the light-

skinned among us "fair" and still refer
to "good" hair and whenever those we
reflexively call "white
lady" feel free
to call a grown mature
black woman old enough to be
somebody's blood aunt
that . . . this . . . the . . .
". . . girl"

Dedicated to my parents' sisters—
Katey, Limi, Aunt Litlee. And,
especially, to my Mama Wawa,
who some presumed they knew as "Aunt Tootsie."

On Free Will and The Rights Of Man

Tall Thomas Jefferson's DNA
is the real writing on the White
House wall, a semen stained graffito:

. . . cry Sally cry
close your anxious eyes
turn to the north
turn to the south
turn to the one with the prettiest
lies in his mouth. . . .

Teenaged "quadroon" Sally Hemings may have
crossed her –
self many times contemplating the slave ships'
blacks' gray sea cemetery
her forebears crossed while she criss-
crossed the old New World Middle
Passage as an African
American serving her master's daughter,
who was her niece.

In the course of human events in Paris
The Founding Father initiated a (38 year)
affair with fifteen year old, relatively
fair Dusky Sally who he owned, and, bye
the bye, by whom he had children. But
today we are told the bright inventor
of the dumbwaiter was, after all, a man
of his time. *Things* were different then
for those of us now up from slavery and down from

Jefferson. When he nightly, tightly,
held his inherited Happiness face to face
did her handsome charms make him tremble
in her arms when he remembered the Self-

Evident truth that . . . *God is just?*

The Founding Father kept her, if not his blood-
stained word, and did not will her free. "Mighty near white...."
Sally Hemings did what she had to

do, day and night, survived her master's
Brotherly Love and died free. Our nation's
Liberty Tree is rooted in her grave. In mind
her headstone reads:

Free at last free....
If you didn't like my peaches
why'd you shake my tree?

Her descendents freely finger desiccated, yellow
pages of a partly executed legacy
printed on dried peach skin peeled off Nat Turner,
reproduced *en masse* and for sale:
facsimile *memento* copies of the *Declaration*.

And right down to today
our oral histories say, not only
did one of our presidents' kids have black
blood, one of our presidents *was* by white Black Codes

a Blood! By the laws by the men of his time.
Idealistic, conflicted, all-
too-human Humanist Jefferson, indeed,
should have, could have, would have

found it *a degradation* that history
has pursued him like a bloodhound;
that hard science has colored the cold, white
lie with a woman's warm, soft, pliant body politic;
her Virginia Bright, tobacco leaf skin; long, straight,
dark ... down her *veiled, black monotony....*

... back by night the brilliant Founding Father
lay with the light black childwoman
who was by white blood his sister-
in-law, but, by *The Rights of Man*
and law, his slave and begot Madison,
Beverly, Harriet and Eston. "Vicissitudes," we are

told, "the way of the world." And we now know all
the wherefores, the whereofs, the whereas
and *Y*. And long ago learned that
The Big House can, indeed, stand divided

against itself and unbecomingly
become The Executive Mansion,
Enlightenment University,
corporate headquarters,
and a neoclassical national shrine.

. . . ride Sally ride
open wide your loving eyes
turn to the north
turn to the south
turn sternly to the one
with The Whitest Lies
in his mouth. . . .

Keeping The Faith

for my great-grandfather, William David Holmes,
Union Army Soldier

We, the late legion American Africans
who fought
for Thee and Thy democracy,
for the dream to come
true, through Thy revolutionary lie,
beginning with first blood, Boston's Massacre,
a cascading
spill which ". . . 'Tis of Thee. . . ,"
begun for those who would try
to run us through, impale us, two
centuries later, on The Heritage Trail,
with our own eagle-pointed flagpole

We hail and salute you!

We, too, the five score and more
thousands of late freed colored,
bronzed in Common Park,
who fought in The Civil War to reaffirm
Liberty and Justice for all, who
learned we fought for Jim Crow, found freedom
was a dispirited Negro
Spiritual, and sang
our red and white blues,
we, the cadenced, columned corps of colored soldiers

We salute you!!

And those of us who chose and did not
choose to serve up our Negro limbs
our nerve and lives
in a segregated military service
during World War Two,
who back then wished for
a little more liberty to defend—

We salute you!!!

And we, the Blacks, the Bloods
who were through with you
by Vietnam, you who
showed us which cheek you'd kick
if we turned the other, you
who in 'Nam would
call us *brother*, but not at home,

We salute you!!!!

And today? Today? Duty?
Booty?

Honor? Or, oil? Country? Or, Kuwait?
Saddam Hussein? The Fruited Plain?
Or, Jesus' Name? Today, come
what may, today we African Americans who are
about to die and don't know why –

We salute you!!!!!

*Note: In ancient Rome, gladiators, many of them from enslaved
or subject peoples, would face and salute the emperor or governor
and say in Latin, "We, who are about to die, salute you!"*

The Music

after reading "All God's Dangers:
The Life of Nate Shaw"

Your archival voice
our long blues song,
life's story
coughed up
the blood-soaked cotton
gag. Blue blood,

Book-long
blue steel guitar blues.

Your Smith and Wesson
.32 gun metal voice.
Six strings.

What did they call you
when you didn't yield?

"If you were
a white man: principled,
mule: stubborn,
nigger: crazy."

You were a blue steel guitar

and your wife was
a fiddle and a tambourine.
Hannah. Soft as cotton
and as strong.
And your wife was
a fiddle and a tambourine
and we your sons are
banjos
and we your daughters
cane fifes.

Playing your gun metal voice,

playing your blue steel
guitar book-long song

CRAZY!

The Last Scottsboro "Boy"
And the Body Politic's Disease

for one of our "strong men"

You might have thought justice
was a jive, cracked tune,
sung with a forked tongue,
like the Liberty Bell's.

But you held life
like a steel guitar, your jail cell
a twelve-bar blues, and strummed it:

All people should be free.

In Alabama, the governor's
pardon, Wallace gives you some skin.
His representative and Miss. Belle
try to ring Liberty, but
it's Alabama
and you know it's a blues tune:

Clarence Norris, aged 63.*
I have no hate;
I like all people.
All people should be
free. I wish these boys
were around to
see . . .

. . . how
those other ruint boys
and they
women
doing down

in Tuskegee.
They disease-free?

*Words of the last of the nine Scottsboro "Boys." In 1976 he was handed Governor
Wallace's "pardon" by the current beauty queen, Miss Alabama. The last of the two
hobo prostitutes who had brought false rape charges against these men confessed on her
death bed that the charges were lies.*

Big Zeb Johnson

Mother's father:
red brown, raw-boned, Virginia born,
Indian Blood, from whom I get my six-four size,
died of diabetes during the White Depression,
leaving three high-strung, violin colored
daughters and Brotherly Love's widow,
Aunt Tootsie, who I, later, as first born,
manchild, grandchild, named Mama Wawa,
who, also sick with "sugar," wound up
worn out, from taking in the world's wash,
waiting for ". . . that Great Gettin' Up Morning. . . ."
sweetly mad, with one leg, in an old
World War One wicker wheelchair and died
of diabetes.

I am because you
unemployed and blue
sugar-blooded, through those old T.B. and pneumonia
times never let the three, not one of their six
small feet, get wet or cold
when the chilling, killing colorless
flakes fell one or two or three feet deep.

You took your knife-edged, steel coal shovel, a pace
ahead of their in-a-row, gosling walking,
and awed eyes gawked, window shades
went up, curtains parted, in witness to such love.
Philly folk watched you dig down to the slate and brick
sidewalks, metal-on-stone sparks and phosphorescent snow,
sun powder, glinting over and around

the firecrowned
big, bent over, upright, steam exhaling, drive-shaft-fast
locomotive of
a man, "going like sixty"
leaning into the labor, fathering,
fathering, the whole long cold mile to school:
"Diabetes be damned!"

Your neighbors came to count on this
courtly care, their kids following yours,
all in a row, those retold winter mornings, so many miles
and years ago. Today, the you in me,

through genes and oral history, speaks
of the gray-haired rigors of the long haul,
going on sixty, as I deal
with my own three, worrisome, brown sugar, teenaged
daughters—and live
with diabetes.

For Joanne Little

I

The Caged Bird sings;

"My Lord, what a morning. . . ."

Gold dust
dawn is the only wealth I have.
August pines
green with haze.
My eyes ache from striped vistas.

Dew on the dead
roaches
come and go more freely than me.
I can't stand them. Stomp them
nightly. County jail
night stomp's the only dance I do.

Grits. I guess

the jailer will try again.
Always eyes my thighs. He may put his key in that
steel lock. But he may not steal,
may not put nothing in me. Not *even.*

Wish I was in Philly. Wish I was a Little Bigger.

Wrinkled, red, half-deal pecker-
wood!
No rusty key for this dusty lock.
Not *even.*

No matrons. He always eyes my thighs, but
I can't hold it forever.

Keys hanging from his . . .
they always offering keys

then changing locks.

Dignity is a key
I'm keeping.

II

The Ice Man:
The blacker the berry . . . yeah
they just naturally love me.
Never say no.
What makes them so agreeable?
What makes them
all good?

Can't remember how much I've had
to carry an ice pick. *You have*
no choice
see? They seem to
be getting stronger. *Struggle*
only make it better. All
of them. Feels better . . . *feels* . . . *yeah*
I bet it's all good . . . all good . . . LAY STILL!!!

III

The Caged Bird:

Feels good to unlock the wishbone,
   to know his death is unlocking
   with this key
   is chipping ice
ribs   and   sinks
          and   sinks
          and   sinks
          and   sinks

   deeper than he did
did
did
did

IV

He falls free
in a puddle of pants,
moans, sighs, rolls
awful eyes around at the dead
roaches dot his naked
thighs.

His death
the open door to
dignity

uncaged

(the only law in this state is Darwin's)

flies.

V

The Police, as chorus:

Must have been wearing a mask;
took it off; changed some;
seems a Little Bigger.

Black. Twenty. An outlaw. Shucks,
y'all get her dead or alive.
Killed a brother Klucks
while he was doing his duty
to our tradition.

(whispers) She's a beauty.
Reminds me my mammy,
bring her in
". . . when the stars begin to fall"
y'all and we'll finish the job
and then book her for murder.

VI

Evergreens. Death is a resin breathed
is in the air
in Carolina.

The Police, as chorus:

Was wearing a mask;
seems changed, seems
a Little Bigger; and,
you know,
so does
every nigger
now.

Fired Up!!

for Judy Rollins

Winnie Mandela got fired from the revolution
today. Her husband fired her over
charges of bribe-taking,
insubordination, charges of insulting
The Queen of England,
whose tourist photo palace was never
bombed,
whose tutored children's grown up matinee,
soap opera lives were never
threatened,
whose womanhood, whose humanity was never
violated, who was never strapped and
tortured
to stay
awake for a week
by electric shock,
charged by static hate, conducted by her own
urine, who never had to take stock of guns,
take charge of a national revolt, a struggle of millions,
and stay beautiful,
giving, giving, giving
her smiling, radiant, defiant persona to a revolution
for a quarter of a century. The Queen

who never raised her own children or genteel, white-gloved
fist in the face of an automatic
weapons-wielding police charge,
without the presence of princely husbanding.

Amandla! The Queen

who never mothered her people
with the blood and blue milk
of a national labor, birth, and afterbirth.
Winnie Mandela, who, while pregnant
with a new nation, lullabyed the fetus with:

We're fired up!
Won't take it any more!!!
We're fired up!
Won't take it any more!!!!

But the government is formed.

Our old, noble, prize-winning Warrior Prince
had high tea with the Queen, who later left for London
and a crown made of melted Krugerrands,
the petrified tears of warrior/women/workers,
the jeweled sweat beads of his nation's minors.

Winnie Mandela was
fired from
the revolution today for rebelliousness,
impropriety, for influence-
peddling, causing embarrassment,
for doing what
she had been asked, told, inspired to do—
for a quarter of a century.

Impromptu: After The Call

for Joanne Gabbin

"The poet . . . is only an instrument
in God's hands."
Kofi Awooner

you call all of us so far
forty out of forty-five
come to the gathering
to be
bound to each other
by sea
crossed history by the mouth
borne black we call
words on white bond we

are mute as the muzzled
storied dead until you open us
silent as still
air stirred to wind that passes
through taut tuned heartshaped mind
turns tongues finger pages
binding strings stitch connections

to winged things flocked
victories high john
some sweet angel chile
homing dawnward
your tears are libations for her
black rose and african violet voices
all those insistent vulnerable sisters
found inside sisters

gone

lost to nothing
passed along ethereal

as breath
tangible as words durable
as the resonating air we call
music we feel you know

we imagine you
think and imagine what it feels like
to be me and more
the us in the u.s.
more the we in I
am because you were
we are and will be

Georgia On His Mind

At the bar
the black man
picks up his glass

the way he picked cotton.
Gin oils Eli Whitney's machine.

His tongue is cotton;
his mind a cotton gin;
his life a mill wheel on
the river, oils the machine.

His soul is a boll weevil.

Red, White And Blues Country

In The Rainbow Grille
(a dark, white bar with a country box)
a rock salt and pepper corn

bearded, tri-colored Blood
in worn camouflage, torn
jeans, wearing broken, deep brown
shades, grimy baseball cap
and old, colorless cowboy boots,

played Cline's "Crazy" over
and over. Spent all his green for
food stamps and rent
on sweet, warming, meriney wine,
chased by burning, fluid amber.
Bought the house many rounds. . . .

Shots

leave him
cold, red-eyed
and blue, fingering the gold bands
and dog tags on the steel bead chain

hanging from his

. . . over and over. The record changes.
The old tone arm moves
from left to right; he stands, stumbles
raises his glass as though to toast
someone, something

Stares.

Muscles jerk. Bent
over, he jukes
the joint, over and over, he hunches
heaving undigested supper,

lunch's sour mash,
corned beef and cabbage,
breakfast's hash, fried egg
on toasted rye. He drops his empty glass.

Glassy stares like shards
in blood red faces
watch it and him, ". . . *go*

to pieces." Someone

says, "Greenie? He was
a two-tour Beret!
Hell, he'll be o.k."

J + 12

for George Singleton

Sees him coming,
puffs,
looks away. Rocks back
and forth to his Reggae.

"Nice day, huh?"

Looks up through steel-rimmed
shades,
nods
and smiles.

". . . Good 'J'?"

Smoke signals. Silence.

"Beautiful, gorgeous day
for getting down on some
Columbian. Or
is it Mexican?
Huh?"

Looks away. Smoke signals.

"Jeez, I talk too much."

Smoke signals.

"Ruining your high, huh?
I understand.
But,
tell me man,
is it from 'Nam?"

Frowns, smokes,
smiles, shakes his head, says

"Your Mom."

Kinda Blue: Miles Davis Died Today

In print you told the world, the first imprint
on your ear's-eye was the tear-
shaped blue gas flame. Its organic funk
from things long dead. The burner's hiss

the sound of an afterlife.

Your indulgent, Garveyite father,
a dentist who didn't shine grins,
spoiled you but saw that you grew black,
saw that you blew blueblack.
Taught you "America."
Taught you personal freedom, like love,
is a twelve bar blues, Dunbar's blue steel cage.
Showed you the way to play in
and the cost of playing out. In The City

caged, bar–bending Bird blew you away,
your mouth agape,
your wide eyes busted grace notes; slack-jawed,
you had no chops for Diz,
and you wallowed in wannabe.

You found your father's blues, found you
rang true, ROUND
MIDNIGHT, at the height of your humanity,
When The City's cops beat you for
being.
You
peeped the stacked deck of union I.D. cards
—for blacks only—pass books
American apartheid, pointed
to the concert hall poster of your Horn-
Of-Africa face, modulated "My Nation
'Tis Of Thee" to, This is me! This is me!!
The night stick played Langston Hughes' hard Bop
on your head.
You bled blue notes

all over your white shirt, your vines
setting yet another trend:
blood-red blues.
Suited you to fit Bubber Miley's mute
to your belled horn, a plunger for the
burnt out throat. Cool, ice blue artifice. You forged split notes
from metallurgy and alchemy of brass, shaped
the tear intense gas blue flame and burned.
Burn Miles! Before the burner's turned off! Cook! You a gas!

Your trumpet's voicing focused baby blue
spotlight on an inner intense tenderness, propane-flame-pure, spare
phrasings from the source of our spirituals
you gave birth to the cool.
Maybe too coolly, muting

rage in a silent way. Putting down
beating up what you loved: you
woman-beating, Coltrane-smacking, Monk-abusing
heart-rending not-so-funny valentine.
Beating up yourself, smacking your own
face with heroin, the near–death blow,
nearly out on Duke's East St. Louis
Toodle O-O-O. Knocking yourself all the way down the dirty dozen
steps to heaven. Self-absorbed, yet
unselfish, generous with what really matters.
You cool!! You bad!! You Miles!!! You "mother. . . . . . ." you
dead but not IN A SILENT WAY.

The Bones And Dust Of The Poet

Though his was a capital voice,
a laurelled life sometimes censored
(but never quieted) by the state
of things, his body lay in
state for reviews more reverent
than his life's work received.

They celebrate his life with death,
the pagan sacrifice of cut tribute
flowers. By daily break-
light they quote his own street weed
words with tongues like the petals
of dying roses, poems perfect as cultivated
pearls for The Poet of beads, sand grains,
wildflower seeds and sweaty hands, serve
as artful, elegant elegies to his antic Etcetera Art.

Once an outlaw poet, he lived
even when joyously jailed, superbly
free to be himself and long enough to see
himself become established—if not establishment.
And, so, adoringly,
at the Talmudic Buddhist Poet's tomb they lay down
chiseled lines, mutter mantras to invoke him, use every-
thing, but no one can sing his dissonant jazz zen jive.
Theirs are fresh-cut long-stemmed words weighed down
with round rhetoric mouthed through his defaced
death masks, their personae purring prayerful
praise of work they had condemned
from podiums, writing they had inveighed
more than they had invested in. They promote
his silence, still. He had been a self-

indulgent sort, "constructively destructive"
someone once said about his urges and impish impulses.
No more than most of us, and perhaps because of us
or for our sake, he had sacrificed himself to sensation.
More a smoker than a fire breather, he had made an incense

of his breath. Now, since laid to rest,
they dig him
up for anniversaries of their causes,
careful, now, not to stomp on his barefoot
free verse. At conferences some wear his words
on T-shirts. At a state university

some about-to-be PhD purloined
The Poet's pickled penis from their Special Collections,
wore it as a pendant
when he wanted to
rite and download him-
self from his pedantic web-site. Others
violated The Poet's entombed tomes, scraped his bones,
ground to powder the desiccated
pages of the body of his work,
and use their index
fingers to write
poems in his
dust.

Bob Kaufman?

No. I did not know him.
But here, in old New Bedford,
I hear New York based, Beignet City born,
baritone, redbone Bob Kaufman was a young
merchant seaman on *The Ancient Mariner*.
In his twenties, in the forties, once or twice
on shore leave here he hung out all day drinking sky

blue moonshine from mason jars passed
around Afro-Luso to Afro-Anglo in befriending
casas or parked cars of Cape Verdean
American fellow National

Maritime Unionists. Or bought rounds
of barroom whiskey to oil their shared lunch
on lore and launched lies at The Crystal Crioulo
Café where there were more *mornas* on the jukebox
than Storyville's Pops Armstrong or Kaufman's heydey
Lady D. They say on shore he was a banned, standup, labor

activist, at sea a damned good deckhand.
That on his off –
time he would bend
his lean frame over the bow, cast his net
of wishes, catch schooling
fish of fancy catch-as-catch-can.
Haul in flitting, quick
silver sardines that glinted dripping sunlight, pull

up florescent daymares *de mer* from the melange bottom.
He would dry and smoke them and pack them
in his head. Called back and forth to California,
to The City by cyclonic causes
of the howling Manifesto Movement, he

left the ocean. Past parts of him are listed
on brittle browning manifests from a middle
passage vessel

---

and German Jewish migrant ship. Banished,
famished for his mother's homecooked, upright music
in their booklined living
room, he fed on free mumbo jumbo, Freud, Cesaire,
Fanon, Kafka, gumbo, goulash and God
knows, man, whatever he could get panhandling.

Otherwise when empty stomached he drank in Bud
Powell's hip echoes of his homestead or toked
smoked dreams. Sometimes he retched our poetic
Rorschach inkblot nightmare, his
life's work, piece by piece:

"What is American to me?"
Perhaps his light rum daemon,
his gin genie overly wrought their work on him,
but nonetheless, he wrote about the U.S.
in us with no "shit" and not a "motherfucker"
among his words. Perhaps he, like a lot of us,

mused too long in hard lit barroom mirrors, saw
and felt us all in him and tried to drown
or numb the taunting lies and truths that stared
him down and out. But Kaufman's *in* again! Why?

Perhaps he was like Miles: self-
absorbed yet kinder to, more loving
of his art form, and, because of that,
more giving of good to all of us than to him-
self or those in his life who loved him? He knew

back then any one of his poems
was more realized in our lives
than the *Declaration* or *The Daily News*.
He knew and wrote America was a *Murder
In The Cathedral*, a rape
in a museum school with moans among
the masks and bones and screams. Silence

he knew, too, was necessary if a jam was to be

heard over the din of institutional lies from
lecterns about: color, lack of color, "race," sex,
gender, power, money, *truth, justice and the American Way.*

Though Bird-like in self-abuse, he was more
the austere, word-play Monk of poetry, sometimes
the sentimental, homespun Erroll Garner. But he was not
some sepia Breton, he was never
"the black Rimbaud." How

could he be? American
as red beans and rice, bagels and Buicks.
Hip as jazz. *Down*
as labor union dues and unemployment

blues. No, man, I did not know him.
But truths in some of Kaufman's poems
remind me, remake me better
understand myself, my context. And that
(aside from giving pure delight)
is one of the best things done

by any poetry or any person.
No. I never met him, but after
The Ancient Rain I hear and see
hungry Bob Kaufman
listening to Birdsong, knelled silence,
black gardenias, and post-Bop, post-Beat,
super-hip/
hop poets, listing to

port and vodka, spouting Eliot, scat-
ting, hopping onto the hood
of a gilled, fishtailed fifties car,
laughing and howling at the croissant moon.

you should be shoo be: amiri baraka

you could no longer just be
an on
going off
beat drop
out poet in a society
that beat up on you but
never in
cluded you be
doo be
doo be
doo besides
in *blues people* you

had jumped off
your cantilevered cool
score for crane's truss "bridge"
over deep river's troubled water

larry walked the talk
with you
thru *black fire*
askia toured you
thru ancient ideograms in father
africa's unrolled papyrus scroll
primer: akan & bambara 1-2-3
        conga (black music)
        dogon ewe fanti 1-2-3
        mojo (black magic) you

picked up down
picking banjoed back to kora
it became you to be
a griot you reigned
as chief america nommo mau mau
imamu you sprung us from the 12
bar blues with good news
about our blackness:

aesthetics ethics should be are
one sister brother a ga "ka ba"
(no mo' doo doo)
adinkra dink a doo

spirit house ensouled us
with renewed black heart
minded home tongue
you gave
us all of you we
gave back our ears eyes
collective word

you could no longer be
just another beat
in the music

you booked from
an angry idyll
angst too
hip for words
& broke bad
you blued red
& white to
green black bloods
you remade your

self african as your own on
call for us to pick up hand carved fist
topped ebony lickin' sticks to drum
a steeled peace for our self

warring selves just up from
wholly stolen cargo people
shipped across holy water
by the dirty dozens
to many thousand hellish places
via the good ship *zong* the *phillis* the *power*
& the *glory*
east to west

left of wright
the body of your work read red (will
never be a corpse &) always
plays the bridge be

tween yesterday & tomorrow:

to truly live you must
be your poetry
which should be is
your politics
your aesthetics
your ethic
your ethos world

view too you
can't just
chant justice you struggle
don't just
say write unity you

need to must
be & do be
more than an imitation of
your imitators' shoo be doo be doo's

& by the dozens hundreds
thousands tens of thousands
we by rite rewrote
our reality renamed ourselves named
our children kamal nneke kalonji
nia kimba ayan reza
thought lived worked word
play clay africanized
the national hive's domesticated doo
be drone bees we became us
on our own heady raw black honey &
x'd old double crosses burned into our brains with cross

pollinated poems

potent stinger pens
to protect ourselves by more
than any dreams necessary

to span the gulf home you
spun ananse's black silk cocoon to keep us
from the tacky white tar
baby's fly paper *declaration*
yankee doodle lie
you webbed the hood with barricades
of barbed wire words
sharp as the *amistad's* cane knives so's
suspension cables of consciousness
from burning cities' melted country
blues steel guitars that played
the bridge so many thousand

crossed over baraka
so long ago
& all along you
so becomingly voice(d) our various
righteous right on power
to the people 60's 70's selves

out of your personal middle

passages you put down the pan pipe
cleared your hudson river reed of self
pith
freely tenored an old call
in another register
another key as we pitched
boxes full of forked tongue tea
leaves off the george washington bridge

you long since wrote all that was
word possible made worldwide earthtoned
connections your discordant choral chords
rearrange received histories'
choke hold languages' sour noted suite

of rum sung barracoon sea chanteys

here's to you for
having borne and delivered so many
of us as
eulogies before our after
elegies praise songs
for yet another invoked dead *bad* blood
spirit for uninvited

(an' aint i a poet)

black warrior women 60's poets
in their 60's & 70's
you walked out on "on" 's
last free verse line left

. . . to live your poetry
with your african/native
american/poet/life
partner you went to the nearby reservation where
you saw read thought about:
    academic bounty scalps
    multicolored indian corn
    nat turner's tanned skin red
    rice recently cut off
    cured blackened rind yellow
    souvenir ears of the empire's
    more recent enemies
    ken sara-wiwa's gavel beaten black
    & blue tongue put in a mason
    dixon jar of crude palm wine refined
    tourists sip from old black gold
    coast scallop shells one american
    oklahoma bomb decades after
    bombed burned down black tulsa killed
    more people than all
    those long burning 60's city summers
    but not as many
    as the 1898 ghost dance

or 1943 camp van dorn
mississippi massacre for national security

TERRORISM IS AS AMERICAN
AS BLACK TESTICLE PIE

the totem of broken word stolen
ideograms penn's indian treaty
lynching tree the pulsing promise
in the masses of unbroken people yesterday

today & tomorrow . . . as always

at each reading you
return to us renewed
stand up before us
blow red white black
and blue facts as gainsay
into the masked face of lone ranger racism
loudly read your "amerika" state

of the black art scat
"cherokee" from here
to "come sunday" hum *home* by way
of our elevated underground railroad
. . . *systems* . . . thru trane's "alabama" modulate "afrika"
to a brassy bravura based
on the internationale
without one corny shoo be doo be doo

Puttin' On The Dog

for "Corner Girl"

Is my shit correct?
Is my vine correct?
Are my kicks country or correct??
Is my "do" down?

Is my shit correct?

Is my rusty black dic-
tion correct?
Should my ever more erudite
utterances be in "The Vernacular?"
Should my presentation be
theatrical and spectacular?

Is my shit correct?

Should my manner be mannered
and laid back??
Is my poetry *Poesy?*
Does it go too far into *haute couture
noire?*
Does it come from hard facts
and Fanon,
or does it refer repeatedly
to *The Canon* trippin'
in *Trickster Mode*, tryin'
to *Trope*-A-Dope?????

Is my shit correct?

But, hey, black poetry's got more
than one good way.
The other day I asked a young Blood
poet if my stuff was correct, if it was
happenin'.

He said, Breaklight becomes dawn,
Ol' Head. The *word* "happenin"
ain't happenin', ain't "where it's at."
Today it's *on*. Word!
Our work is *all that*.

Attitude Adjustment

Yo', Dr. and Ms. C.E.O.,
what's goin' on?
"Multiculturalism?" Well and good.
But don't stop there! How does that empower

us down in the 'hood? How
is that an end? Just
like you did back in the day,
you say you care.

You provide opportunity for us
to fete our films, our food, to parade
our style, flair, our dance and ethnic hair.
Like back in the Harlem Renaissance

or, not too long ago,
when we wore dashiki
and 'fro. Yeah, it's all good
for any generation.

Even so, it's no substitute for
political self-
determination. Thought we learned
it ain't nothin' but a means

to an end, an amends, interlude. Other-
wise we are left behind
without institutional power
or our own authority, with
only our color -
ful neo-Negritude, Latinotude,
Arabitude, Indianitude,
Asianitude—
and an ongoin' attitude!!

The In-Dex

Right on
the end of the predawn
Nightside Business News Brother Dexter's one
of the boys. With his crescent grin,

starry eyes, he's suited for the job in smart, conservative,
powder blue, red tie, white shirt.
No doubt
of The Party of Lincoln

and for Colin Powell
For President.
Standing in
for the system

in the inside
marble balcony on the wall
of The Stock Exchange.

His mahogany hand cradles
the gavel. He dexterously handles, grabs
it, smartly pounds
it on the block.

The black-face image of the auctioneer who trans-

ferred his great grandmother
from handler to handler.
Though he was born through concentric cervixes,
out of her Middle
Passage, Dexter is borne
above it all.

Clamoring bull rallies
before and after
the clanging of the closing
bell brings down the business
of yesterday. Again,

he brings down the gavel
. . . down in the hold
down to The Delta
down on the thin knee
bone soup of prayer, the blues
of black mothers' milk. . . .

Up in the neoclassical
lapis lazuli balcony
Dexter's in like a fat rat.
Dexter's

down.

To Be Or Not To Be

Want to "make it" in America?
ACCOMMODATE the inequities
of your oppression.

ASSIMILATE genteel genocidal
eurocentricity at Multiversity U.

CELEBRATE your color-
ful, quaint lack of power and
authority with cathartic, forked

tongue dialogs, "ethnic" fashion shows
of designer clothes, self-
dis-
plays, chilled wine, cheese and cracker
buffets.

DEMONSTRATE BUT DON'T
AGITATE the powers that be.
Become schooled
in their dictates
and you will be cool
as cash, closed mouthed
as quiet money.

ROMANTICIZE the way the masses
around the world have been
and are institutionally knocked
down, knocked up, kept
down, stepped on and stepped

over by the upper classes
and their agents, the true
big dog git ovah gangstas:

conquistador
missionary

                    colonizer
                    slave holder
                    robber baron
                    generalissimo
                    c.e.o.
                    president
                    board chair.

BE FUNNY about five centuries
of nullified *negroes*, four centuries'
sold lots of three/fifths human
beings. Be hilarious about "bad" hair,

                    brandings
                    lynchings
                    rape
                    castrations
                    experimentations
                    hard *de facto* facts
                    brutal, lethal service
                    and protection blues.

COLLABORATE. Buy into The System
that eats migrant workers for bread:
grape, bean, lettuce, and apple
pickers, underpaid, overworked,
ununionized southern female fish
house workers and "illegal" ones
from Central America who fell through
NAFTA's net to our up-
lifting, fishes and loaves, crumby,
under-the-table, life-threatening work

"ethic." Invest in down-
sizing megamergers that leave u.s.
meager workfare jobs making hamburgers.

APPRECIATE a century of kindly quotas.

EQUIVOCATE recent years of negative action,

"reverse discrimination" rhetoric reaffirming
supremacy of the national myth:

"DON'T WORRY

BE HAPPY!!

We will do you
the inalienable right
thing out of our fair
mindedness, out of the goodness
of our historical hearts.
Have we not put true
red, WHITE, yellow, brown and
black-and-blue on you
for hundreds of years?
Put your fears behind you.
No need now to legislate
compensation, allowance nor
reparation for holocaust—
at least
not for you."

BE CIVIL about *all that*
and "universal," too.
Pursue your happiness
by any (unjust) means
necessary.

APPROPRIATE. And you just might
be a limited (undeserving) "success"
and live LARGE unserving
in this mass mess
we all call America.

Dominion

X's on black baseball caps
are bull's eyes in gangsta

     turf wars'
     cross hairs

and at meetings of the new
militias of The Old Cause

Undoing The Do

for Darrel

Yes, as we have sung,
we *are* overcoming
and have come a long way
to get where we are
today.

But we are not beyond
The American Rite
of right-wing, night-riding
racism. Rightfully,

we rap; we brag on
how we are
survivors. Yes. We
have survived; some
few among us even flourish.

To survive
the horse-dragging,
car-dragging centuries'
social hells we had
to adapt to them
by light of church

and cross burnings
in our souls. Adapting
to hells so well
some to some ex-
tent have emerged
from them some-

what hellish from the history,
by grand design. In mind
self-
generating slaves

salving festering sores
with the calming balm of THINGS.

So as we remember
Martin Luther King and
sing We Shall Overcome,
we need to free
our designedly
fractious, ununited

selves
from escapist narcissism.
For ourselves we need
to ask why we want,
we "need" to
live LARGE, instead

of "abundantly."

Why
we feel we need to
buy, to own, to drink,
to drive, to use,
to dye, or bleach, or fry,
or straighten

some of the things
we do and why we do
some of the things
we do to and with our-
selves and one another.

Pop Pop

Why

so many
old black
men's brown
eyes

blue,

too

?

. . . Here . . .

In memory of my great-grandmother,
Martha Prattis Nichols Brown,
who lived to be 111 years old.

for Ayan

She rose from the rocker, unfolded
The Afro American article,
Pointed it out:

Lord!
This world's a mess! Folks fighting to be
called "Most Oppressed":

black folk, women folk, old folk.
Who's most oppressed? Me I guess.
Got it all, being
as I'm old, black, woman.
But, so what? Whining never
got even a kid more than candy or
a pat on the head, nor a yard dog
a kick or a bone.

Struggle and strife are the facts of life.
Your hard working Grandpa's dead, but
you are the afterlife of his labor.
Our work has been our worship.

So, take our tattered, threadbare, patchwork
hope and work with it. Yes, kneel to God,
but stand up to people who fight your right
to the life God give you.

Some say "home is where the heart is."
That's true if heart is courage, strength and faith.
'Cause, in this life home is wherever
your struggle is. And, son, the work's undone.

We just cleared the ground, plowed and planted;
the weeding, watering,
watching, waiting, the long work
is up to you. We ain't no ways through.

So, yes, keep the faith, but
keep the farm, too. Hold on
to home ground, and learn that living
should be learning, too. Remember
what Fred Douglass read and wrote for you,
and Robeson, your Malcolm X and Dr. King.

The main thing written clear
Right 'mongst these headlines here:
The whole world's your home, hear? Here. . . .

AT THE ACCESS

Occasionally

for Maya Angelou,
Marge Piercy, Joe Gouveia, Corey Cokes, Megan Tench,
and the other poets gathered at Angelou's Cape Cod residence,
August 13, 2000

Do you write every day?

Yes, I do, out of cut off
dreams, by breaklight,
birdsong and dusky dawn.
But let me say right

away, whatever
writing may come from the daily rite
is not always poetry, not even blankly.
No more so than are all

pop rap's rhymed lines, nor every
effort in the antique norms called
verse forms. But when I ken, I can
write poetry. The real thing slowly rises
through me then. And, as I often say, if

after rewrite after rewrite
I end my work hours with
one strong, tight page of poetry
or three prime pages of prose,
God knows, that's a good day!

Can I get that copy of your book
from you? You *may*. But you may not
"buy it" nor "get it," even if you do.
Once you read it through
you may not agreeably take my take on life.
But I will give it to you anyway.

You see, we poets are brothers, sisters

in the craft of a vocation, a calling,
a way that chooses us.
We keep our word by giving it away.
What is any of it anyway, but how
with words we tender responses
to our window paned predecessor's
decomposed longhand world,
a still life still

seen in the sand; his watercolor angels??
Or how we devine
the dried, brittle Yarmouth beach rose
pressed
between
the watermark pages of his self-
illustrated *Auguries*?

Or recollect the collective personal
dream – from which we all fall or rise – named
history? Or respond to the miracles
mundane as mothers milk? To blood-
hounding adversity? What

but our written reactions to fallow love,
close-cropped loves, term-love's harvest,
or love plowed under????
So we plod in the furrows of our brows
throwing seed words toward life freely grown.
By reading them to the wind with our taxed

and metered breaths we sow them in the cracks
and faults of each other's being. Being
liberating agents we endow, we try
to give the ordinary agency to be,
again, heightened, memorably.

From some source by which we rise having been
drawn down to it as sailors are to the sea
from which all lives and deaths and lives
have come to this. The long way

to say, yes, I write every day.

On the other hand, poetry comes
to and through me occasionally. When?
I say again, when I keenly ken, I can,
by the dawn of dusk by sounding my own
deep or fitful sleep,
by any dreams necessary.

The Moose: First Sighting

It is Everything

out here! A manifestation of Divine Mind,
this largest American
deer with horse-sized legs and torso,

head just raised. Living,
leafed greens hanging from its horizon-
wide antlers, lake water

draining from its long, side-to-side chewing,
oddly mule-like mouth. All of the great ungulate animal out-
lined,
auraed by its cumulus exhalations.

Looking

for all the world
like a cloud webbed, mountain landscape with peaks, low,
brown piedmont, wet, green woods with waterfall. Suddenly
falls

prey, in echoing report, to the Constitution
righted, sharp-sighted, high-powered NRA bullet. . . .

. . . The Indigenous "Great Spirit" sinks in a dying body
of Adirondack acid rain water. Blooded, generationally,
our Old Republic rises in an inanimate lakescape
wilderness that has been

bleeding since the first cut
out plot of "private property";

expiring since the first life and death
territorial, tête-a-tête, war painted face
off between tomahawk, birch bark canoe,

musket ballshot and man-of-war.
A mandamned wilderness flooded red
with sunset, with arcane sportsmanship,
the sanctity of Father-to-Son

first kill/first blood rites
and inhumane Enlightenment

Human Rights.

At The Access

in loving memory of my parents,
Everett and Estelle Hoagland

The view is always renewed. Today
as I descended the weathered steps of the lake
access, I paused to look at shadowed Champlain
—and remembered
"Points Of Interest" in the staid, old Essex Inn's
new brochure: the bay is four hundred feet deep
far out, off nearby Town Park Beach. At the bottom
I wondered

who walked in, fell in, jumped in, went
under to lake bed long ago. Who drowned
among the Native Peoples, early French,
the sport fishermen, canoeing tourists,
heedless, headstrong children? Whose

were the accidental deaths, recurrent,
despairing suicides? Something unseen
splashed. The whispering water's low waves, ripples,
lapped the pebbled shore distorting my reflection
as I stood there barefoot, ankle deep, on the edge

I sank
into deep, dark, cold silence; a sullen
city frame of reference made the mirroring
water more than forty stories deep. . . .

. . . A black loon surfaced,
a small shiny fish sideways
in its beak; shook its feathers dry;
shook and headfirst swallowed its stilled, quick-
silver prey.

The wind picked up; the hardwoods' new leaves showed
their silvered undersides. The pines swished hushes
overhead. A brown duck's alarming squawk
and sudden flight across my bay

of years to boyhood, across the centuries
settlements, aboriginal millennia, the glacial lake's ice
ages and thaws brought me to see me
and the water for what we were, what we are, what we will,
can be, again, all that. I gazed at, contemplated
Champlain's tiered mountain backdrop.

Squatted, searched,
picked up a thin, flat stone; watched it skip
the water over and over and over again after
my windup and curled-finger pitch, skills—
like bike balance, fishing, swimming
—learned for life.

I stared across the great lake and heard the silent
visual fugue of Vermont's undulant Green
Mountains; pushed off
taking tackle box and other gear; rowed
my little childhood boat
toward them across the suddenly still waters
and hummed a hymn.

The Pilgrim

Up from the bottom, the basin, up
from the four hundred feet deep,
great, glassy lake unlocked by Seaway. . . .

. . . Away from the dark water's reflection
of my face, by way of pseudopodia,
across the alluvial plain above
the pebbled shore. Up the dawn-lit upland's

wild, star flowered, allotted acres, cast
lots by dew light over the overgrown field-
stone fence chinked with chipmunks. . . .

Past the past's antique, white, shotgun houses. Past
caroling robins up in the gnarled, barren branches
of the Old Garden's blistered apple tree. Just to be
hardbitten by

big June breeding, protein-needing, black Adirondack, blood flies.

But somehow, by someway, up-
standing, straight backed, sure footed in the salving
stream of noon sun beaming down and all around
the sloped length of hard-won clearing. . . .

Slowly ascending the low, shadowed piedmont,
up into clearer air, through
the last stand of old growth pine, to sit
on top of glacier-cleft escarpment long

gone Indians' tongues termed Split
Rock. Its degenerating boulder base
surrounded by crumbling
stones. . . . Inspirited, still

looking up, staring into, searching
the starry night sky as one

searches his/her new baby's face, as nursing
babies take in their mamas'
faces, up there, out there where

all the above, all that below
and I began. From here
on the mountain peak the lakes look
like the great, rainfilled foot-

prints of a god. I turn
around and see The Other's track
merge with mine. I return
to staring up at the end

-less, time-
less Thing,
one of the ones
all of us stare at:

ocean, great lake, camp fire, hearth fire,
mountain, Milky Way, our newborn's face,
searching, sensing, seeing,
hearing the spiritual, and from what, from
where and how we have come

to be.

...Unfinished...

for Darrel,
forever....

myth miracle math

scientists have more reason
to be spiritual   higher
mathematicians the cryptic

poems called
equations   their theories ultimately
seek to understand what seems to be-

come of mass space gravity energy radio
galaxies more profuse than all of earth's atoms
change   astrophysicists must imagine conjure
mundane miracles   metamorphoses

with divinations like arcs of light
with handfuls of hard facts held fast
as insects in amber   fossil

fish in broken loaves of shale
the flesh made text   outlines
of life and death on slate tablets brought down

from weathered mountains   bones that can be read
in rock   answers easy as gases ashes
to ashes to life from black hole

born of the
boon of the
egg

yolk sun dust water greens pollen honey milk
dreams reveal more and more

mystery

in deep sounding whales psalms
   O out of the resounding silence
out of the endless black whole
infinity eternity

   O wholly holy

The Author

Everett Hoagland has been a busboy, a factory worker, a truck driver, a part-time longshoreman and a full-time educator for thirty-five years. Hoagland was born and raised in Philadelphia, Pennsylvania, but New Bedford, Massachusetts has been his adopted home since 1973. For the past twenty-eight years, he has been an English professor at the University of Massachusetts' North Dartmouth campus.

Professor Hoagland teaches poetry, writing and also has created five different, ongoing African-American literature courses at UMass Dartmouth. He has been a published poet since his undergraduate years at Lincoln University in Pennsylvania, where Langston Hughes, a Lincoln University alumnus, took the time to sit with him and go over two of Hoagland's early manuscript poems. This encouraged Hoagland to take his own poetry more seriously, and he graduated with Lincoln's annual creative writing award.

In 1968 one of his poems was anthologized in Clarence Major's book, *The New Black Poetry*. In 1970 historic Broadside Press published *Black Velvet*, the second of Hoagland's four chapbooks. The collection was perhaps the first collection of Afrocentric love poetry authored by an African American and published by a trade publisher with national distribution. Several of the collection's poems were included in Bantam publisher's 1970 anthology, *The Black Poets*, edited by the late Dudley Randall, which remains in print and still is widely used on college campuses.

In 1971 Hoagland was awarded a University Fellowship by Brown University to pursue a master's degree in their graduate creative writing program. Poet Michael S. Harper was his thesis advisor, and Hoagland graduated in 1973.

Since then, Hoagland's poetry has appeared in literary journals such as *The American Poetry Review*, *The Massachusetts Review*, *The Iowa Review*, *The Beloit Poetry Journal*, and *Cross Cultural Poetics*. Other periodicals that have published his work include *Essence*, *The Progressive*, *Communications Education*, *Longshot*, and the nation's oldest African-American magazine, *The Crisis*, the journal of the NAACP. In the 1970's the poet was a frequent contributor to the important (but now defunct) periodicals, *Black World* and *First World*.

Newly published anthologies that contain recent work by Hoagland include *The Body Electric* (W. W. Norton publishers), *The Garden Thrives*

(Harper/Collins), and *The Jazz Poetry Anthology* (Indiana University Press).

He has received the Gwendolyn Brooks Award and twice he has been awarded Massachusetts Artist Foundation fellowships.

Hoagland recites a poem (after interviewing Kalama ya Salaam) on the Black Arts Movement program "The Furious Flower", four videos of African-American poetry produced by California Newsreel and produced and edited by Dr. Joanne Gabbin.

From 1994 to 1998 he was the mayor's designated Poet Laureate of New Bedford. In 1998 Hoagland's poem about Frederick Douglass' escape from slavery in Maryland to freedom in New Bedford, titled "Just Words," was the choral text of Andrew McWain's "Symphony of Just Words". It premiered with The New Bedford Symphony Orchestra, a choir of 250 voices and professional soloists, at the Zeiterion Theater in downtown New Bedford, as part of the dedication events for the official opening of New Bedford's Whaling National Historic Park.

Hoagland continues to be invited to read his work to audiences all over the United States and in other countries, most recently at the University of Ghana in West Africa and in Havana, Cuba (with a translator).

Hoagland's first full-length volume of poetry, *THIS CITY and Other Poems*, was published by Spinner Publications, New Bedford (spinner@ultranet.com).

He can be contacted for poetry readings at: (508) 999-8286 or write to:

P. O. Box 7463, New Bedford, MA 02742. His email address is: ehhoagland@AOL.com